Loving Your Neighbors

Stonecroft

All Scripture quotations, unless otherwise indicated, are taken from the Holy Bible, New International Version®, NIV®. Copyright ©1973, 1978, 1984, 2011 by Biblica, Inc.™ Used by permission of Zondervan. All rights reserved worldwide. zondervan.com The "NIV" and "New International Version" are trademarks registered in the United States Patent and Trademark Office by Biblica, Inc.™

Scripture quotations marked (NLT) are taken from the Holy Bible, New Living Translation, copyright ©1996, 2004, 2007, 2013, 2015 by Tyndale House Foundation. Used by permission of Tyndale House Publishers, Inc., Carol Stream, Illinois 60188. All rights reserved.

Scripture quotations marked (ESV) are from The ESV® Bible (The Holy Bible, English Standard Version®), copyright © 2001 by Crossway, a publishing ministry of Good News Publishers. Used by permission. All rights reserved.

Illustrations by franzidraws

Designed and Typeset by Serena Lilli Jeanne

Written by Janice Mayo Mathers

ISBN: 978-0-9908500-8-3

Produced and Distributed by:

10561 Barkley, Suite 500
Overland Park, KS 66212

800.525.8627 / connections@stonecroft.org

stonecroft.org

© 2017, Stonecroft, Inc. All rights reserved. The right to use any portion of this book may be secured by written permission.

The views, opinions, and positions expressed in this book are those of the author and do not necessarily reflect the views, opinions, or positions of Stonecroft.

Contents

Acknowledgments — 1
Introduction — 3

Section 1: **Getting the Vision for Your Neighborhood**
    Your Sphere of Influence — 8
    Loving with Words and Actions — 14
    Moving Out of Your Comfort Zone — 18

Section 2: **A Compelling Difference**
    What Speaks the Loudest — 26
    The Allure of Consistency — 32
    The Appeal of Sincerity — 38

Section 3: **Our Prayers in Action**
    The Bold — 46
    The Beautiful — 52
    The Persistent — 56

Section 4: **Our Hearts Awakened**
    Avoiding Discouragement — 64
    The Importance of Discipleship — 70
    God's Pursuing Love — 74

Group Prayer List — 79
Leader's Guide — 81
Who is Stonecroft? — 83
Resources — 85
Notes — 87

Acknowledgments

When it comes to writing, nothing worthwhile happens without a team. So many different people have been an essential part of the *Loving Your Neighbors* team – praying, editing, designing, marketing – that to assign one name to the final product is a bit misleading. I am so grateful to Stonecroft, the epitome of teamwork, because in everything they do, God is the source of their inspiration and vision. The ultimate "thanks" goes to God for empowering our team to produce *Loving Your Neighbors*. May He be glorified through this book and in the lives of all who read it.

– Janice Mayo Mathers

Introduction

The days ahead are going to be exciting. Our neighborhoods are full of people searching for God's love and truth in turbulent times – and we have what they need. In this season, God is inviting us to love our neighbors as ourselves (Matthew 22:39) as we pray and point them to a saving relationship with Jesus Christ.

Jesus provided clear direction for living well in community. Some people found His teaching riveting while others were baffled or shocked. The religious leaders of Jesus' day felt threatened by His power. The more they tried to discredit Jesus, the more curiosity He aroused in people.

Putting their well-educated minds together, the religious leaders devised questions designed to trick Jesus into committing blasphemy. They questioned Him on divorce, remarriage, payment of taxes, the resurrection – every subject for which they had established strict laws. But the truth and wisdom of Jesus' words constantly outwitted them.

One day, after listening to the ongoing debate between Jesus and the religious leaders, one man asked Him the ultimate question: "Of all the commandments, which is the most important?" Imagine the silence that settled over the crowd as each person awaited His answer. So many laws restricted their society. Which would Jesus put at the top of the list?

"The most important one," Jesus replied, "is to love the Lord your God with all your heart and with all your soul and with all your mind and with all your strength" (Mark 12:30). Love God above all else. It wasn't a surprising answer given the importance of religion in that culture. But what Jesus said next probably surprised everyone. "The second is this: 'Love your neighbor as yourself.' There is no commandment greater than these" (Mark 12:31).

We love God because He first loved us (1 John 4:19). The overflow of that love pours through us and influences our neighbors. It's the demonstration of God's love and kindness that draws unbelievers to repentance (Romans 2:4).

One way to cultivate God's heart for your neighbors is to pray for them. Prayer helps us grow in compassion and understanding and gives insight into what God is doing in the lives of people He puts on our path. Each section of this study offers prayers to help you live out God's great commandments to love Him and those around you. It also includes Scriptures to meditate on and space to write your reflections about praying for and reaching your neighbors with the Gospel.

So, gather a group of women and meet where it's most comfortable. As you go through the study together, get ready to see God move in answer to your prayers! Whether you already have a good relationship with your neighbors or are just getting to know them, expect God to provide new opportunities to share the Good News. His love is contagious. May it spread to schools, businesses, government offices, and every part of the community He set you in for such a time as this.

SECTION 1:

Getting the *Vision* for Your Neighborhood

Your Sphere of Influence

Where you live and work is not an accident. God knew you would be part of that community, and He has a plan to use you for His purposes. Your "neighborhood" may include your street, workplace, local grocery store, or any affinity group to which you belong.

As we get started, take a moment to define your neighborhood and write in the space below the names of specific neighbors who come to mind.

_____

_____

_____

As you pray for these people, ask God to give you a real love for them and concern for their well-being. Ask Him for insight and discernment as you interact with each of them. Ask Him to fill you with a winsome boldness as you begin this adventure of praying for your neighbors.

"We are brought together because of Christ's invitation, and the people he puts us alongside of may well be the very selection of neighbors we have been avoiding all week."[1]

– Earl Palmer, noted Bible teacher and pastor, quoting author C.S. Lewis

It's not always easy to love well. You may be thinking right now of a neighbor you would rather avoid. The good news is we don't have to muster up love and kindness in our own strength. As we pray and seek God's heart, He gives us grace to reflect His nature and character to others. He can even soften our hearts for the most difficult and challenging people we know.

So, get ready for God to work in ways that will amaze you. Heaven is in the process of being enlarged because of your commitment to this journey!

SCRIPTURE FOCUS

"And then he told them, 'Go into all the world and preach the Good News to everyone'" (Mark 16:15, NLT).

Karen stood at her living room window looking at the 11 houses circling the cul-de-sac where she lived. Her mind went back in time to another cul-de-sac she and her husband had moved into. She remembered surveying the daunting stacks of boxes the movers had just unloaded when the doorbell rang. On her doorstep stood a woman with a brilliant smile and a plate of cookies. "Hi! I'm

Renee from next door," the woman said, handing her the cookies. "I just wanted to say welcome to the neighborhood!"

That day was the start of a transformation that left Karen forever changed. Although she and Renee were miles apart on nearly everything they talked about, there was something about Renee that Karen found compelling and comforting. One day Renee invited her to a luncheon. On a whim, Karen accepted. At that luncheon, she heard the Gospel for the first time.

Recalling the profound difference Renee made in her life, Karen looked at the homes in the cul-de-sac where she now lived and wondered, "Do they know Jesus?" As Karen stood at her window, she began praying for each of the families. She prayed for their marriages, for their children, and for their physical, spiritual, and emotional welfare.

The next morning, she stood at her window again, praying for her neighbors. For six years, she continued to pray for her neighbors every day, asking God to bless each family, to open their hearts to Him, and to give her opportunities to talk with them.

One Christmas season, Karen invited the women over for a holiday tea. All 11 women showed up. After the tea, she handed them an invitation to a Bible study in her home. To her amazement, all 11 women accepted her invitation. Karen realized this was an answer to six years of prayer and that she shouldn't be so surprised. God had been preparing their hearts, just as He had prepared her heart through prayer. And just like her, all 11 women were changed forever as they committed their lives to Jesus Christ.

The importance of sharing the Gospel with those around us, as Karen did, is emphasized in the last words Jesus spoke on this earth before ascending to heaven. They were words of commissioning that still apply to followers of Christ today: "Go into all the world and preach the Good News to everyone" (Mark 16:15, NLT). As we do this, Jesus promises to be with us always, to the very end of the age (Matthew 28:20).

Sometimes the thought of personally putting the Great Commission (Matthew 28:19-20) into practice is intimidating, isn't it? When you think about this in terms of your neighbors, what concerns you the most?

Write those concerns below.

_____

_____

_____

_____

Reflect on God's promise to be with you. How does that speak to the concerns you wrote down?

Keep in mind as you use this prayer resource that God loves the human race. He created us. He is so passionate about us that He went to the extreme of sacrificing His only Son, Jesus Christ, in order to bridge the chasm of sin that separated us from Him. It is an inconceivable price to pay, yet that's the depth of God's love for us.

Take a moment and ask God to make this truth real to you regarding each of your neighbors. Let the image of Christ on the cross form in your mind. Imagine His eyes searching out the neighbors for whom you are praying.

What thoughts come to your mind?

God placed within our fallible hands the invitation and responsibility to spread the word of His remarkable love. As we grow in relationship with Him, He helps us live in such a way that people around us want to know the God we know. He empowers us to represent Him well so that others want what we have.

As you think about the image of Christ on the cross and His love for your neighbors, imagine yourself in the picture. Imagine His eyes locking on yours as He whispers, "I brought these people to you."

How will you respond to His personal commission to you?

SCRIPTURE FOCUS

"For God in all his fullness was pleased to live in Christ, and through him God reconciled everything to himself. He made peace with everything in heaven and on earth by means of Christ's blood on the cross" (Colossians 1:19-20, NLT).

Prayers for Yourself

Father, make me aware of the Holy Spirit's power within me. Compel me to be Your witness to the people in my sphere of influence (Acts 1:8, NLT).

Thank You, Father, for giving me the Holy Spirit as an Advocate who teaches me everything I need to know and reminds me of what You have said (John 14:26, NLT).

Lord, out of Your glorious riches, please strengthen me with power through Your Spirit so that Christ will dwell in my heart through faith. Give me the power to grasp how wide and long and high and deep Your love is. Let me know this love that surpasses knowledge and fills me to the measure of all Your fullness (Ephesians 3:16-19).

Prayers for Your Neighbors

Thank You, Lord, for coming to seek and to save my neighbors who don't yet know You personally (Luke 19:10).

Father, thank You for Your Son, Jesus Christ, who can save completely those who come to You because He always lives to intercede for them (Hebrews 7:25).

Lord, I know You can do immeasurably more than all I could ask or imagine in my neighbors' hearts and lives and that Your power is working in me, too. May the Holy Spirit draw my neighbors to You (Ephesians 3:20).

Reflections

What is God showing me today about my relationship with Him?

What is God showing me today about my relationship with my neighbors?

SECTION 1: GETTING THE VISION FOR YOUR NEIGHBORHOOD

Loving with Words and Actions

Jesus said to love God and love your neighbor as yourself. The two commandments are connected. In other words, the way we love our neighbors reflects a measure of our love for God. Let that sink in for a minute. Do your words and actions show a strong love for God? Is your concern for those around you the same as it is for yourself?

To further emphasize the point, Jesus used the word "neighbor" to refer to "any other person, irrespective of nation or religion, with whom we live or whom we chance to meet."[2] The fact that this commandment is repeated several times in the New Testament underscores its importance. Both Galatians 5:14 and Romans 13:9 tell us that the entire law can be summed up in one phrase: love your neighbor as yourself. When we set our hearts to do so, we begin to live as God has called us to live.

What are some ways you can love your neighbors through both words and actions?

_____

_____

_____

_____

It's been said, "People don't care how much you know until they know how much you care." This is especially true when it comes to sharing our faith. Our neighbors need to see Christ reflected in our interactions with them before our words will carry weight. Our actions, conversations, and prayers open the door for influencing our neighbors for Christ. And before our words resonate, our actions speak volumes.

As you think about this, do you need to let go of any grudges or mend any fences with neighbors? Do you need to change any attitudes so you can repair or build good relationships with them?

_____

_____

_____

_____

The most important counsel of God can be summed up: "Love God and love your neighbors." In fact, Jesus said all the law and the prophets hang on these two commandments (Matthew 22:40). Christian author and theologian John Piper says this about the daunting commandment to love our neighbor as we love ourselves:

> It seems to demand that I tear the skin off my body and wrap it around another person so that I feel that I am that other person; and all the longings that I have for my own safety and health and success and happiness I now feel for that other person as though he were me.
>
> It is an absolutely staggering commandment. If this is what it means, then something unbelievably powerful and earthshaking and reconstructing and overturning and upending will have to happen in our souls. Something supernatural. Something well beyond what self-preserving, self-enhancing, self-exalting, self-esteeming, self-advancing human beings ... can do on their own.[3]

It is not possible to live out this kind of radical love in our own strength. It takes God working in a supernatural way through our words and actions. As we prayerfully submit to His leadership, this kind of love can transform our neighborhoods. It just takes willing hearts and yielded vessels. God is zealous to do the rest.

SCRIPTURE FOCUS

"'Love the Lord your God with all your heart and with all your soul and with all your strength and with all your mind;' and, 'Love your neighbor as yourself'" (Luke 10:27).

"The commandments, 'You shall not commit adultery,' 'You shall not murder,' 'You shall not steal,' 'You shall not covet,' and whatever other command there may be, are summed up in this one command: 'Love your neighbor as yourself.'" (Romans 13:9).

Prayers for Yourself

Father, help me to never bear a grudge or seek revenge against my neighbors. Instead, help me to love them as I love myself. I know this is possible as I follow You and trust Your leadership in these relationships (Leviticus 19:18).

Lord, may I let no debt remain outstanding except the continuing debt to love my neighbor, because when I love others I am fulfilling Your law (Romans 13:8).

Father, let me remain in Your love and keep Your commandments so that Your joy will be in me and my joy will be complete. Help me to follow Your command to love my neighbors just as You have loved me (John 15:9-12).

Father, keep unwholesome talk from my mouth and help me to say only what will build up my neighbors. Help me to be kind and compassionate, forgiving them just as You have forgiven me (Ephesians 4:29-32).

Prayers for Your Neighbors

Lord, help my neighbors to hear Your Word and believe in You so that they may cross from death to life and spend eternity with You (John 5:24).

Lord, show my neighbors that salvation is a grace gift of God that comes through faith, not by works. Lead them to accept Your gift of salvation (Ephesians 2:8-9).

Lord, stir my neighbors to call on Your name so they will be saved (Romans 10:13).

SECTION 1: GETTING THE VISION FOR YOUR NEIGHBORHOOD

Reflections

What is God showing me today about my relationship with Him?

What is God showing me today about my relationship with my neighbors?

Moving Out of Your Comfort Zone

When the recession of the 1980s hit, Sherry's family found themselves unemployed and forced to relocate. They left their home in the country where space was plentiful and jobs were scarce and moved to an inner-city apartment where space was scarce but jobs more plentiful. Instead of wide-open fields, their two sons had concrete and blacktop for a playground. Instead of rabbits and coyotes for neighbors, they had prostitutes and drug dealers. Sherry was so overwhelmed with settling her family safely into their unfamiliar surroundings, she had little energy left to consider the spiritual well-being of her neighbors. Her greatest concern was protecting her children.

One morning after sending her sons to school, Sherry heard a knock at the door. It was a woman from the apartment across the hall. Sherry and her family often heard the sounds of fighting coming from that apartment and saw two subdued children slinking in and out to school.

The woman's face was strained. When Sherry invited her in, she blurted, "I know you must be a Christian because I watch your family leave your apartment every Sunday morning. I don't have any food for my children and wondered if you could help me."

Sherry realized that just leaving their apartment every Sunday had been a witness to her neighbor. After this encounter, Sherry started thinking about her other neighbors as well and how she could step out of her comfort zone to reach them. Her kids were making friends with many children in the neighborhood, so she decided to have a "Bible Snack Time" in her apartment. While Sherry fixed some healthy snacks, she sent out her sons to invite the neighborhood children over. Soon her living room was filled weekly with children enjoying snacks and listening to her Bible stories.

Because of the Bible Snack Time, the mothers started coming for coffee, sharing their problems, and asking for advice. Sherry continually took risks to build relationships with women whose lives were drastically different from hers. Every time she opened her door, she was ready for God to use her to spread His love to her neighbors.

Can you relate to Sherry's initial hesitation in reaching out to her neighbors? Maybe you've felt overwhelmed or unsure where to begin.

In what ways does the idea of reaching out to your neighbors feel uncomfortable or risky? Write your thoughts here.

_____

_____

_____

_____

God understands everything you just wrote down. He knows your personality. He knows your neighbors. He knows how to prepare their hearts for your words. In fact, He already knows their response! Take what you wrote above and turn it into a prayer. Ask God to give you the grace and boldness you need to take the next step. Ask Him to open doors to relationships with your neighbors. It just takes one willing person for God's love to ignite a neighborhood.

One of the most vivid examples of God's transforming love is found in the encounter between Jesus and the woman at the well (John 4:1-42). The story begins when Jesus' disciples leave Him sitting by a well to rest while they search for food. While they are gone, a woman from a nearby village comes to draw water for herself. Right away, Jesus is fully aware of her need. Most people didn't draw water in the heat of the day; they waited until evening when temperatures were cooler. Clearly, the woman wanted to avoid her neighbors.

No doubt Jesus also noticed her hardened and worn appearance that silently proclaimed her brokenness. He could have ignored her as most others did, and surely she would have preferred that. Instead, Jesus moved beyond cultural norms of the day and struck up a conversation.

"Would you give me a drink of water?" He asked.

The woman couldn't believe this Jewish man was talking to her, a Samaritan, given the strong prejudice Jews had against Samaritans at that time.

What should I do? Is He trying to trap me? she may have wondered.

After asking for a drink, He told the woman He could give her living water that would quench her thirst forever – quite a claim since He had no means of drawing water at that moment. When she responded that she wanted some of that water, Jesus suddenly switched subjects – first to her marital status and then to religious practices.

Her mind must have been whirling, trying to keep up with the conversation, and yet she found Him irresistibly compelling. She couldn't stop talking with Him. "I know that Messiah (called Christ) is coming," the woman said. And then came the words that changed her life forever: Jesus declared, "I, the one speaking to you – I am he" (verses 25-26).

The disciples returned just in time to see the woman drop her water jug and run toward her village in excitement. Now the woman was compelled to take a big risk. Forgetting what people thought about her, forgetting her reputation and low social standing, she called to her fellow villagers to come and see the Messiah. Because of her courageous witness, "many of the Samaritans from that town believed in [Jesus] because of the woman's testimony" (v. 39).

God's Word, the truth of the Gospel, is compelling and contagious. If you are willing to share it, God will make sure it fulfills His purposes in those who hear it.

SCRIPTURE FOCUS

"As the rain and the snow come down from heaven, and do not return to it without watering the earth and making it bud and flourish, so that it yields seed for the sower and bread for the eater, so is my word that goes out from my mouth: It will not return to me empty, but will accomplish what I desire and achieve the purpose for which I sent it" (Isaiah 55:10-11).

Prayers for Yourself

Father, You have taught me to put off my old self and to be made new in my attitude, to put on my new self that is created to be like You in true righteousness and holiness. Now enable me to speak Your Word with great boldness (Ephesians 4:22-24, Acts 4:29).

Lord, You have chosen and appointed me to go and bear fruit that will last. Today I ask that, according to Your will and in Your name, You will use me to help my neighbors begin a relationship with You (John 15:16-17, 1 John 5:14-15).

Lord, help me to live my life in a way that is worthy of the calling You have given me. Make me more humble, gentle, patient, and loving with my neighbors – especially the ones who are most unlike me (Ephesians 4:1-2).

Lord, since I have been purified by obedience to Your truth, help me to love my neighbors sincerely and deeply, from my heart (1 Peter 1:22).

Prayers for Your Neighbors

Father, I pray that You will have mercy on my neighbors. I pray You will save them through the washing of rebirth and renewal by the Holy Spirit so they might be justified by Your grace and become heirs with the hope of eternal life (Titus 3:5-7).

Thank you, Lord, that Your arm is not too short to save even my most broken neighbors when they turn to You. Soften their hearts today to receive the truth (Isaiah 59:1).

Reflections

What is God showing me today about my relationship with Him?

What is God showing me today about my relationship with my neighbors?

SECTION 1: GETTING THE VISION FOR YOUR NEIGHBORHOOD

SECTION 2:

A

Compelling

Difference

What Speaks the Loudest

*T*yler had just gotten his driver's license and savored the feeling of freedom that accompanied the small piece of plastic now residing in his wallet. He was thrilled every time his mom asked him to go to the store. On one such errand, he detoured through the car wash, then cruised through town with the windows down and his favorite music blaring from the speakers. This was the life!

Tyler picked up the items on his mom's list at the grocery store and climbed back in the car. After checking his rearview mirror and backing out of the parking space, he heard – "smack!" The sickening screech of crunching metal turned his legs to butter as he got out of the car.

The first thing he noticed was a Christian bumper sticker on the car he'd backed into. He felt some relief. "At least the driver will be kind," he thought. But the furious woman emerging from her car did not live up to the words on her bumper. She screamed in outrage, her language peppered with vile and vulgar words. She even used God's name as a swear word. In a subsequent call with Tyler's parents, she apologized for her behavior, but for Tyler, her actions spoke louder than the bumper sticker or her apology.

The title "Christian" carries a negative connotation for many people today. It is often synonymous with words such as judgmental and hypocritical. As unfair as we may find such labels, the truth is we often inadvertently live up to the stereotype.

These inconsistencies tend to justify the label "hypocrite." In his book, *Fresh Power,* Christian author Jim Cymbala addresses this issue: "Instead of engaging this world and proclaiming the gospel of God's love with an accompanying manifestation of God's power, as we find in the Bible, [we are] reacting in one of three ways:

1. Running away from the world, circling our wagons, and saying, 'Isn't it horrible the way people are living out there?'

2. Making harsh and condemning statements about the world and its people, forgetting that they are not our enemy but rather our mission field.

3. Letting the world 'evangelize' us without our realizing it.'"[4]

This type of reality check is often uncomfortable, but necessary. Take a moment and ask God to show you how you might be contributing to the world's negative opinion of Christians.

Which of the three reactions listed on Page 26 do you most identify with and why?

_____

_____

_____

_____

_____

Now consider this: God has called us to live blameless and pure, children of God without fault in a warped and crooked generation (Philippians 2:15). He asks us to do this so that we will "shine like stars" to the world around us. How might this feel like an impossible task? Before answering, note that it says blameless not sinless. There is a difference.

Blameless as it is used in this verse means unmixed or unadulterated. In other words, our lives in Christ should not be mixed with the sinful deeds and actions of those in the world. God doesn't expect us to be perfect or to avoid unbelievers. He just doesn't want us to conform to the sinful patterns of this world (Romans 12:2).

How does Romans 12:2 say we can live transformed lives? How does this truth help us live in alignment with Philippians 2:14-15?

Philippians 2:15

So that you may become blameless and pure, "children of God without fault in a warped and crooked generation." Then you will shine among them like stars in the sky.

Romans 16:19, NLT

But everyone knows that you are obedient to the Lord. This makes me very happy. I want you to be wise in doing right and to stay innocent of any wrong.

_____

_____

_____

_____

Our minds are renewed – or corrupted – by what we put into them. The Apostle Paul instructs us to be wise about what is good and innocent about what is evil (Romans 16:19). The truth is we are affected by various influences such as books, movies, music, social media, television, and other forms of entertainment. The more we meditate on what is pure, lovely, admirable, excellent, and praiseworthy, the better positioned we are to shine the light of Christ to our neighbors (Philippians 4:8).

How can we make sure we are in the world but not of the world (John 17:16)? It helps to remember that God's mercy took us out of darkness into His wonderful light, and His Spirit in us enables us to live out that truth in our sphere of influence. As God's beloved daughters, we are encouraged to abstain from sinful desires, which wage war against our souls (1 Peter 2:11).

If we're honest, this daily charge is challenging, to say the least. How can you practically apply this instruction to your life? What area would you most like God's help with?

Turn that desire into a prayer.

_____

_____

_____

_____

The more we identify with Christ, the greater our strength to resist temptation. In other words, if we're on a diet it's a good idea to stay out of bakeries! Peter puts it this way: "Live as free people, but do not use your freedom as a cover-up for evil" (1 Peter 2:16). It is very easy to use our freedom in such a way that it ultimately wages war within us. This can lead to choices that compromise the freedom we have in Christ and our witness to others.

Take a moment to examine your life socially, financially, professionally, physically, and emotionally. What kind of citizen are you? Are there any entertainment habits you feel God wants you to change? How well do you manage your finances? What is your reputation as an employee, employer, or co-worker? How do you emotionally deal with life's ups and downs? Are you a conformist – pretty much living as everyone else does – or are you being transformed?

When thinking about our influence on others, we need to realize it is true that actions speak louder than words. So, as God transforms you, share your journey with your neighbors. This type of Christlike living has the power to transform them, too.

SCRIPTURE FOCUS

"Do not conform to the pattern of this world, but be transformed by the renewing of your mind. Then you will be able to test and approve what God's will is – his good, pleasing and perfect will" (Romans 12:2).

Prayers for Yourself

Father, don't let me ever forget that it is You who works in me in order that I may fulfill Your good purpose (Philippians 2:13).

Lord, help me to go through my days without grumbling or arguing, so that I may become blameless and pure, Your child without fault in this warped world. Let me always shine like the stars in the sky as I hold firmly to Your Word of Life (Philippians 2:14-15).

Lord, give me the strength to be wise about what is good and innocent about what is evil (Romans 16:19).

Prayers for Your Neighbors

Lord, let my neighbors come to the place where they declare with their mouths, "Jesus is Lord," and believe in their hearts that You raised Him from the dead, so that they will be saved (Romans 10:9).

Lord, help my neighbors to understand that it is by grace they can be saved, through faith – and that this is not from anything they do, but it is Your gift – not their efforts, so that no one can boast (Ephesians 2:8-9).

Reflections

What is God showing me today about my relationship with Him?

What is God showing me today about my relationship with my neighbors?

The Allure of Consistency

In her book, *Like a Pebble Tossed*, Jean Zeiler writes about a co-worker named Ivan. She knew Ivan was a Christian by two seemingly small actions: He kept a Bible on his desk that he read during breaks and he prayed over his sack lunch. Every single day. A very shy, quiet man, Ivan never verbalized his faith to Jean or their co-workers; he just lived it consistently, day in and day out.

"I watched him like a hawk," Jean recalls, "just waiting for him to forget to pray over his lunch one time so I could say, 'Aha! You're no better than the rest of us.'" But Ivan never faltered.

Ivan's work as an engineer was impeccable and one morning Jean asked him for some specs for a project she was drafting. "Just off the top of your head," she said, "I don't need it to be exact right now." But Ivan never worked "off the top of his head" and he reached for his engineering book. "Oh, he's got to check his Bible first," Jean teased as the other engineers laughed. Ivan looked her in the eye and said quietly, "This is not my Bible, Jean." Although she didn't fully understand why he felt so strongly about his Bible, she felt terrible for making fun of something Ivan valued so greatly.

Jean's feelings of guilt turned into curiosity about Ivan's commitment to his Bible. She went to a bookstore on her lunch hour that very day and bought a Bible for herself. She showed it to Ivan when she got back to work and he smiled. "May I make a suggestion, Jean? Start with the book of John," he said.

Jean read straight through John's Gospel that very night. Then she turned to the beginning of the Bible and kept reading. In a matter of days, she'd read the entire Bible, riveted by the message of love woven throughout. It wasn't long before Jean found herself kneeling by her chair, asking God to transform her life.

Jean was as bold as Ivan was shy. Because of Ivan's quiet but consistent witness, Jean eventually traveled around the world telling others about Christ. Ivan shares the credit for every one of those souls who now have a personal relationship with Jesus Christ.[5]

This story paints a beautiful picture of how God uses all personalities to make His Word known. The consistent, silent witness of an introvert can speak just as powerfully as the charismatic words of an extrovert. God creates each of us in unique and remarkable ways to play a part in His Gospel story.

Honorable behavior does not need to be justified and cannot be argued against. This kind of consistency and integrity is easy to recognize because it sets us apart. In what ways has God created you to uniquely reach your neighbors for Christ with a consistent witness and message? What are some ways you can demonstrate honorable behavior to your neighbors? To spark your thought process, note what the following verses say:

Luke 6:29

Matthew 7:12

With these verses as a model, how should we respond to people who are inconsiderate, rude, unfair, or deceitful?

Under what circumstances does God require us to look out for others with the same level of concern we have for our own well-being?

Both these verses provide direction for behaving honorably with our neighbors. As you look at your current relationship with your neighbors, what areas need improvement?

Truly, living our lives by the standards Jesus modeled for us goes against our human nature. Yet the more consistently we reflect His image, the better able we are to influence others. In much the same way that Jean became curious about Ivan's faith in Jesus Christ, our neighbors will become curious about our faith as well.

SCRIPTURE FOCUS

"By myself I can do nothing; I judge only as I hear, and my judgment is just, for I seek not to please myself but him who sent me" (John 5:30).

Prayers for Yourself

Father, help me to do to others whatever I want them to do to me, because I know this is the essence of all that is taught in the law and the prophets (Matthew 7:12).

Lord, let me follow Your teaching to love my enemies, to do what is good to those who hate me, to bless those who curse me, and pray for those who mistreat me. Let me be willing, when someone slaps me on one cheek, to offer the other cheek also. If someone demands my coat, let me offer them my shirt also (Luke 6:27-29).

Lord, I know that because I am strong I have an obligation to bear the weaknesses of those without strength, and not to please myself. Help me to please my neighbor for his good and to consistently build him up (Romans 15:1-2).

Lord, because of the endurance and encouragement You give me, allow me to live in harmony with my neighbors with a united mind and voice. Help me to accept my neighbors just as You accepted me (Romans 15:5-7).

Prayers for Your Neighbors

Lord, let my Christian neighbors be renewed in their minds and let them put on their new nature, created to be like you – truly righteous and holy (Ephesians 4:23-24, NLT).

Lord, create in my neighbors a clean heart, renew a steadfast spirit within them (Psalm 51:10).

Lord, save my neighbors, not because of their deeds, but according to Your mercy. Give my neighbors new life and new birth through Your Holy Spirit (Titus 3:5).

Reflections

What is God showing me today about my relationship with Him?

What is God showing me today about my relationship with my neighbors?

SECTION 2: A COMPELLING DIFFERENCE

The Appeal of Sincerity

Want your neighbors to know you truly care? Show a sincere interest in them. Let's be honest. It's flattering to have someone want to know more about you and take the time to really listen. For this reason, your genuine interest in your neighbors may help them open up to you.

In his book *Just Walk Across the Room*, Pastor Bill Hybels tells about dragging his garbage can out to the curb one cold winter evening. Intending to dash out and come right back in, he didn't take time to put shoes on first. He got his can to the curb and turned for a fast sprint back inside when he noticed his new neighbor across the street dragging his garbage can to the curb. Simultaneously, God nudged Bill to go introduce himself to the man. So, he did – bare feet and all. He dashed across the street, held out his hand and said, "Hi! I'm Bill." The man shook his hand, introduced himself, and then they both turned and went back into their homes. That's it! No lengthy conversation, just a friendly exchange of names, and a subtle message that says, "I noticed you there. I care." After that first meeting, however, Bill began to intentionally take his can to the curb every Tuesday night when his neighbor did the same. Over the span of a year, with God guiding him, Bill made a concerted effort to get to know his neighbor, extending their curbside chats longer and longer. In the process, the two men developed a real friendship. The result of those curbside chats was that the neighbor and his family became believers.[6]

Amazingly, when God is at the forefront of your mind, anything can become a means of connecting with your neighbor – even garbage!

In his book *Reimagining Evangelism*, Rick Richardson says that the connecting point with our neighbors is simply "our shared humanity, our common struggles and sufferings, needs and longings." He notes that when we strip away our differences – education levels, social status, talents and experiences – we are all the same. That sameness gives us the opportunity to connect.[7]

Think about the daily or weekly routine and rhythm of your life. Where do you see opportunities to be in sync with your neighbors?

What are some of the ways you can establish a connection with them?

_____

_____

_____

_____

In the early days of Stonecroft, founder Helen Duff Baugh traveled across the United States starting evangelistic groups in small communities. She later wrote about that time, saying, "Farmers were always happy to explain to us about their different types of cattle and crops. In fishing villages, we became well-acquainted with the various types of fish to be found in the area and how to prepare them. In logging communities, we learned much about the woods. And all the time we were making friends so we could introduce them to our Best Friend, Jesus Christ."[8]

Mrs. Baugh was intentional about getting to know the people she met in these communities. She asked sincere questions and listened to their answers with genuine interest. She got them to talk to her rather than listen to her, finding ways in which she could relate to their lives and livelihoods. She kept listening and praying until they were ready to listen to what she had to tell them about Jesus.

Showing sincere interest in your neighbors requires an intentional investment. The return on that investment is priceless. Consider how much you have invested in getting to know your neighbors.

Do you make it a priority to listen more than you talk when you spend time together?

_____

_____

_____

The Apostle Paul gave us a great example of how to establish a point of connection with people from whom he was miles apart spiritually and philosophically. Reading about his mission trip to Athens in Acts 17, we see how deeply saddened he was by all the idols cluttering the city (verse 16). The Athenians had erected shrines to every god imaginable – even an unknown god, just to make sure all their bases were covered. While he was there, Paul took daily walks around the city, talking with the people he met. In the process, he rubbed shoulders with well-educated philosophers who spent their days in deep discussions (verses 17-21). Some scoffed at what he had to say; others were intrigued.

These walks gave Paul a platform from which he could share more about God. When he got up to speak, Paul was careful not to criticize them as idol worshippers. Instead, he spoke to them with respect – even complimenting them. "People of Athens! I see that in every way you are very religious. For as I walked around and looked carefully at your objects of worship, I even found an altar with this inscription: TO AN UNKNOWN GOD" (verses 22-23).

Paul's next move was brilliant. He used the idol to an unknown god as an opportunity to witness about the one true God. He told them he knew who the "unknown" god was – that He was the God of the Universe, who loved them and sent His Son to die for them.

As Paul illustrated, criticism is never a good means of connecting with someone. Neither is passing judgment. Rather than condemning the Athenians, Paul recognized their thirst for spirituality, skewed though it was. He made that need his connecting point. In doing so, he pointed them to God the Father who would quench their eternal thirst.

Considering the differences between you and your neighbors, what are some areas that could become connecting points?

What are some things in common you have discovered with your neighbors?

___

One of the best ways to develop a connecting point with someone is to first pray for him or her. Through prayer, God enables us to see others through His loving eyes, free from condemnation. As this happens, you will notice you are beginning to sincerely care more for your neighbors. In fact, you have probably already noticed a change in your feelings for them since you began using this prayer resource. Take a moment to reflect on how God is moving you through this journey.

Jot down some things you have noticed.

___

SCRIPTURE FOCUS

"If I speak in the tongues of men or of angels, but do not have love, I am only a resounding gong or a clanging cymbal. If I have the gift of prophecy and can fathom all mysteries and all knowledge, and if I have a faith that can move mountains, but do not have love, I am nothing. If I give all I possess to the poor and give over my body to hardship that I may boast, but do not have love, I gain nothing" (1 Corinthians 13:1-3).

Prayers for Yourself

Father, because I have been washed, sanctified and justified in the name of the Lord Jesus Christ, by Your Spirit, let my behavior consistently reflect that truth (1 Corinthians 6:11).

Father, let me be obedient to Your command to love my neighbor. Let me always remember that just as You have loved me, so must I love my neighbor (John 13:34).

Father, help me to set aside any unhealthy desire to "get even with" or "teach a lesson to" my neighbors. Let me be willing to leave them in Your hands (Romans 12:19).

Father, help me to turn the other cheek when my neighbors offend me. Help me to cultivate a spirit of generosity toward things of mine they use or borrow (Luke 6:29).

Lord, above all else, help me to love my neighbor deeply, because Your Word tells me that love covers a multitude of sin (1 Peter 4:8).

Prayers for Your Neighbors

Lord, through my behavior let my neighbors come to see that You are the Light of the World. Let them choose to follow You and never walk in darkness again, but accept the light of life You want to give them (John 8:12).

Father, let my neighbor seek You while You may be found; let her call while you are near. Let my neighbor choose to forsake her unrighteous ways and thoughts. Let her turn to You, so that you will have mercy on her and freely pardon her (Isaiah 55:6-7).

Thank You, Lord, that You are forgiving and good, abounding in love to my neighbor when she chooses to call to You (Psalm 86:5).

Reflections

What is God showing me today about my relationship with Him?

What is God showing me today about my relationship with my neighbors?

SECTION 2: A COMPELLING DIFFERENCE

SECTION 3:

Our *Prayers* in Action

The Bold

When we boldly share the Gospel of Jesus Christ, the Holy Spirit will inspire us. We have nothing to fear, because He will give us what we need in the situation. The truth is that Jesus is more concerned about your neighbors' eternity than you are. He gave up His life to bring them into relationship with Him. He will help make sure the right words come to mind through the power of the Spirit.

Consider the example of bold inspiration found in Acts 3. A man who was lame from birth lived his life in total dependence on the people around him, even depending on someone to carry him out to beg each day. Can you imagine a bleaker future? And then one day this hopeless man encountered two courageous men.

Their names were Peter and John. At first glance, they looked no different than all the others who had passed by the beggar on the street day after day. But when he begged Peter and John for money, they spoke the words that changed his life forever. "Silver and gold I do not have," Peter told him, "but what I do have I give you. In the name of Jesus Christ of Nazareth, walk" (Acts 3:6).

Walk! This one word carried with it evidence of bold faith. Peter believed that this man could do the impossible by the power of Jesus Christ.

The reaction of those who witnessed the miracle was exactly what you'd imagine: a rub-your-eyes-to-make-sure-you-were-seeing-correctly awed excitement! However, when some of the leading authorities arrived and assessed what was happening, their reaction was not so enthusiastic. The priests, captain of the temple guard, and Sadducees were disturbed by what Peter and John were teaching the people, particularly the resurrection of the dead in Jesus (Acts 4:2). They had Peter and John arrested and hauled off to jail. The next day the rulers, elders, and teachers of the law met in Jerusalem to question Peter and John about what happened. They asked, "By what power or what name did you do this?" (Acts 4:5-7).

Read Peter and John's response in Acts 4:8-12.

Acts 4:8-12, NLT

⁸ Then Peter, filled with the Holy Spirit, said to them, "Rulers and elders of our people, ⁹ are we being questioned today because we've done a good deed for a crippled man? Do you want to know how he was healed? ¹⁰ Let me clearly state to all of you and to all the people of Israel that he was healed by the powerful name of Jesus Christ the Nazarene, the man you crucified but whom God raised from the dead. ¹¹ For Jesus is the one referred to in the Scriptures, where it says,

'The stone that you builders rejected has now become the cornerstone.'

¹² There is salvation in no one else! God has given no other name under heaven by which we must be saved."

According to verse 8, who inspired Peter with the response he offered? Who did Peter credit with the beggar's healing?

Consider the heart-pounding stress of this moment. Peter and John were in a terrifying position. They knew the authorities were going to charge them with heresy, which could result in their execution or, at the very least, a severe beating and imprisonment. If they relied on their own strength, it would be extremely hard to think clearly under such circumstances. But Peter and John trusted the Holy Spirit to intervene. And that's exactly what happened! The Holy Spirit put the right words on Peter's tongue at exactly the right time.

Never doubt that the Holy Spirit will do the same for us. He will give us the words as we make ourselves available. He will enable us to speak despite our fear and hesitation. He knows what our neighbors need to hear and will speak through us. What a privilege to be used in this way!

It's normal to feel nervous, hesitant, and even afraid when sharing the Gospel. When we move at God's direction despite our weakness, He will move by His mighty power.

You may have experienced this personally. If so, recall how that felt and record your thoughts here. If not, what do you think this would look or feel like? Why is bold faith important in reaching our neighbors?

Peter, in his defense, described the miraculous healing that caused such a ruckus as "an act of kindness" done in the name of Jesus Christ (Acts 4:9-10). The authorities called it heresy. With the healed man rejoicing right there in front of everyone, it was challenging for authorities to defend the stance of heresy.

While being questioned, Peter saw an open door to share the Gospel.

Empowered by the Holy Spirit, he said, "Jesus is 'the stone you builders rejected, which has become the cornerstone.' Salvation is found in no one else, for there is no other name under heaven given to mankind by which we must be saved" (Acts 4:11-12). After establishing the miracle for what it was – an act of kindness – he gave full credit to the power of Jesus Christ. Not only that, but he explained that they could find salvation through that very same power. Challenging, disarming, convicting, encouraging, awakening. Amazing power is held in a handful of Holy Spirit-inspired words!

The result of Peter and John's run-in with the authorities could almost be classified as another miracle. They were released! The authorities realized they had no choice but to release them. In doing so, they commanded them to stop speaking or teaching in the name of Jesus (verse 18).

How did Peter and John respond in verses 19 and 20?

Can you imagine such boldness? Rather than nodding their heads in relief and hightailing it out of there before the authorities could change their minds, Peter and John chose to defend the truth again. They couldn't help themselves and had to speak up once more.

Have you ever felt such boldness? Recall a situation in your life where you couldn't keep quiet but had to speak up for what was right in the name of Jesus. How does your passion for Christ compare to Peter and John's?

Peter and John set a high standard for sure, but we can ask God for the same level of boldness. The key is to prayerfully trust God and take the next step as the Holy Spirit prompts us. Peter and John's interaction with the authorities shows us the natural result of boldness – more boldness. When Peter and John reported to their fellow Christians all that had happened, everyone joined together to pray for similar boldness (v. 29). God answered their prayer, filling everyone with so much of His Spirit that the building they were in actually shook (v. 31). Just imagine! Doesn't this whet your appetite for prayer? Don't you want to feel that same power moving through you?

As if this story of miraculous healing and boldness wasn't enough already, we've skipped over the most exciting part. Go back and note what happened in Acts 4:4 as a result of Peter and John's witness.

Does it amaze you that the number of those who believed increased to about 5,000? How many neighbors are you praying for currently? Does it seem possible that your entire neighborhood could respond to God through your prayers and interactions with your neighbors? There's no doubt it can happen through God's power and by His will.

Acts 4:4, NLT

When we feel overwhelmed by this call, it's good to stop and meditate on God's truth. Imagine each neighbor's face. Now envision each person coming to know Jesus Christ in a personal way. Picture the joy radiating from their faces as their lives are transformed. Write a faith declaration describing what you are expecting from your commitment to pray for your neighbors.

But many of the people who heard their message believed it, so the number of men who believed now totaled about 5,000.

What is your most daring hope?

_____

_____

_____

_____

Christian author and evangelist Anne Graham Lotz describes becoming a grandmother in her book *The Joy of My Heart: Meditating Daily on God's Word*. "My husband and I are totally enthralled with this little girl. She fills our hearts! We can't help talking about her to anyone who will listen. I'm not afraid to talk about her. I don't plan in advance how I will talk about her. I don't worry about offending someone with my talk about her. I don't go to classes to learn how to talk about her. I don't read books on how to talk about her. I hug that little girl, feel her snuggle up against me, touch her soft cheek, and melt! Little Ruth Bell fills my heart! And what fills my heart comes out on my lips!" she writes. "Why do we seem to make speaking up for Jesus so complicated? If He fills our hearts, He is going to come out on our lips!"[9]

SCRIPTURE FOCUS

"As for us, we cannot help speaking about what we have seen and heard" (Acts 4:20).

Prayers for Yourself

Thank you, Lord, that in all things I am more than a conqueror through You who love me (Romans 8:37).

Lord, it doesn't make sense to light a lamp and then cover it or shove it under the bed. No, it should be set up on a lamp stand so those who enter the room can see their way. Help me shine the light of Your love to my neighbors instead of keeping it a secret. Don't let me hide my relationship with You. Help me bring it out into the open (Luke 8:16-17).

Father, help me always be prepared to give an answer to everyone who asks me about the reason for the hope that I have in You. Help me do this with gentleness and respect (1 Peter 3:15).

Lord, help me to be strong and courageous in talking about You to my neighbors. Do not let me be afraid, because I know that You go with me. You will never leave me or forsake me (Deuteronomy 31:6).

Lord, I know that You have not given me a timid spirit, but one of power, love and self-discipline (2 Timothy 1:7).

Father, because of my hope in You, I am very bold (2 Corinthians 3:12).

Lord, let me proclaim Your kingdom and teach about the Lord Jesus Christ with all boldness and without hindrance (Acts 28:31).

Lord, I pray that whenever I speak, words may be given me so that I will fearlessly make known the mystery of the Gospel (Ephesians 6:19).

Prayers for Your Neighbors

Lord, give my neighbors discernment to know that You are the one true living God – the way and the truth and the life (John 14:6).

Lord, thank You for the example in Acts of the man's healing that opened the door to share the Gospel. I ask you to heal my sick neighbors in the name of Jesus Christ as a witness of Your love and power. Miraculously open doors to share the Gospel with them (Acts 4:8-12).

SECTION 3: OUR PRAYERS IN ACTION

Reflections

What is God showing me today about my relationship with Him?

What is God showing me today about my relationship with my neighbors?

The Beautiful

Even though she found the idea intimidating, Lori began praying for an opportunity to talk to her neighbors about Christ. Unsure where to begin, she focused her prayers on the woman who lived directly across the street. Nervously, she asked God for boldness and opportunity.

One day Lori received a letter from a women's ministry director at a church in another state. The woman had contacted her previously about speaking for their women's retreat and this letter served as written confirmation. A personal note was attached:

> Lori,
>
> Unless your town numbers their street addresses very differently from ours, I'm thinking you must be the neighbor of my college roommate and dearest friend in all the world. If this is the case, how wonderful if she came with you to the retreat. She doesn't yet know the Lord ...

Isaiah 52:7, NLT

How beautiful on the mountains are the feet of the messenger who brings good news, the good news of peace and salvation, the news that the God of Israel reigns!

God is just waiting for our willingness. As we've explored previously, He will create the means for us to make the connections and He will put the words in our mouths. What's more, He calls those who bring the Gospel message "beautiful." Look at how Isaiah 52:7 captures this image.

God sees us – our feet – as beautiful when we bring the Good News of Jesus to our neighbors.

As you look at that verse again, what are the different ways it describes God's message?

_____

_____

_____

_____

It's amazing, isn't it? Such a wonderful description! When you feel intimidated by the idea of sharing Christ with someone, look at it from the perspective of this verse: you are bringing them good news. You are bringing them the means of finding peace and salvation! You are introducing them to the God who reigns over all.

Mike and MaryAnn always used the same florist when ordering flowers for their clients. As they walked out of the shop with their flowers after each visit, the florist would say, "God loves you and so do I!" Mike and MaryAnn were not Christians, but somehow those words always made them smile.

Theirs was a blended family, each of them bringing two kids into the marriage with the resulting challenges. The biggest challenge came from the oldest child, Jim, who was fighting drug addiction. Jim kept their home in chaos as they struggled to build one family from two fractured ones. Just when Mike and MaryAnn felt they were making progress, it would all blow up in their faces.

One night all of them were playing a game together. Everyone was having a good time and it felt like their dream of being a family was becoming a reality. MaryAnn got up to get some more soda from the kitchen and suddenly something slammed into her head from behind. Stunned, she turned to see Jim, his hand raised to strike her again. In a daze, she heard the other kids screaming, heard Mike calling 911, and saw the blood on her hands.

Where do you turn when your son attacks you? Who can help you find the way back from such trauma? These questions haunted Mike and MaryAnn in the days following Jim's unprovoked attack. They had no support system in place for something like this, no friends who could relate. Only one person came to their mind: the florist who always ended their conversations with "God loves you and so do I."

They went to her shop, not to order flowers but to ask for help. She invited them to church, and the very next Sunday Mike and MaryAnn gave their hearts to Christ. Their journey from brokenness to wholeness is ongoing, but in God's eyes they are beautiful – their feet are beautiful as they continue walking their path, encouraging others to join them, including their children.

SCRIPTURE FOCUS

Therefore, my beloved brothers, be steadfast, immovable, always abounding in the work of the Lord, knowing that in the Lord your labor is not in vain (1 Corinthians 15:58, ESV).

Prayer for Yourself

Father, let me never forget the trustworthy saying that You came into the world to save sinners, of whom I am the foremost (1 Timothy 1:15).

Lord Jesus, let Your love compel me, because I am convinced that You died for all (2 Corinthians 5:14).

Father, use me to bring good news and proclaim peace and salvation to my neighbors (Isaiah 52:7, NLT). Father, give me opportunity to share with my neighbors that you did not send your Son into the world to condemn the world, but to save the world through Him (John 3:17).

Prayers for Your Neighbors

Father, I know that my neighbor cannot see Your kingdom unless he is born again, so use me to help bring him spiritual sight (John 3:3).

Lord, help my neighbors understand that You are the atoning sacrifice for their sins, and not only for theirs but also for the sins of the whole world (1 John 2:2).

Father, let my neighbors understand that You are not a God of disorder but of peace (1 Corinthians 14:33).

Lord, don't let the message of the cross be foolishness to my neighbors who are perishing, but may they come to know it is Your power to save them (1 Corinthians 1:18).

Lord, help my neighbors realize the depth of Your love for them – that while they were still sinners, You died for them. Help them see their need for salvation through You (Romans 5:8).

SECTION 3: OUR PRAYERS IN ACTION

Reflections

What is God showing me today about my relationship with Him?

What is God showing me today about my relationship with my neighbors?

The Persistent

Two men lived in a small farming community in eastern Oregon. Both men were prominent in the community. Both were very committed Christ-followers, but they had radically different reputations. When asked about one of the men, others would consistently respond: "He's the reason you'll never see me in church!" When asked about the other man, people said, "If you ever see me in church it will be because of him."

Both men were persistent in their witness, but their neighbors responded to them in completely different ways. Why? One preached, while the other listened. One judged, while the other walked alongside his neighbors. One repelled those around him, and the other drew people in.

Luke 18:1-5, NLT

[1] One day Jesus told his disciples a story to show that they should always pray and never give up. [2] "There was a judge in a certain city," he said, "who neither feared God nor cared about people. [3] A widow of that city came to him repeatedly, saying, 'Give me justice in this dispute with my enemy.' [4] The judge ignored her for a while, but finally he said to himself, 'I don't fear God or care about people, [5] but this woman is driving me crazy. I'm going to see that she gets justice, because she is wearing me out with her constant requests!' "

A persistent witness is just as important as a bold and beautiful one. In fact, they go hand in hand. Bringing God into conversations each time the opportunity arises – not in a forced way, but a natural way – keeps the subject open and ongoing. It also reveals how your relationship with Jesus Christ is inseparable from who you are and how you live day to day.

But the wrong kind of persistence can negatively affect those we're trying to reach for Christ. Have you ever had someone drone on and on about a subject for which you have no interest? How do you react when this happens? Do you tune out and look for a way out of the conversation?

It's not pleasant, is it? The person is essentially carrying on a one-way conversation and all your receptors shut down. They are talking at you instead of with you. Your instinct from then on is either to avoid the person or avoid the subject when around him or her. This is not the type of persistent witness we want to have as Christ-followers.

Take some time for honest reflection. If people tend to walk the other way when they see you coming or keep glancing at their watch while you're talking, make a personal note to adjust how you communicate. Remember the goal is to talk with them, not at them.

Jesus tells two parables back to back in Luke 18. At first glance they appear unrelated, intended for two different audiences. But a closer look reveals something different. Read verses 1-5.

Take a moment to record in your own words the key point in this passage about the persistent widow.

_____

_____

_____

_____

Persistence paid off, didn't it? Now notice the key point in the next parable in Luke 18:9-14.

This parable about the tax collector is all about attitude, isn't it? An attitude of humility. The difference between compelling persistence and repelling persistence is attitude. Our attitude in the midst of our persistence determines how people respond to us. It wasn't the sinner Jesus criticized; it was the religious person.

We want to cultivate a compelling persistence based on our sincere concern for our neighbors' well-being – because that kind of persistence pays off. Joelle is a perfect example of godly persistence. When Joelle's son introduced her to his new girlfriend, her heart sank a bit.

"Beth was not exactly the kind of girl I'd imagined for my son," Joelle said. "And as we became more acquainted, my concern deepened."

Beth's only knowledge of God came from the cult her parents had belonged to when she was a child – a cult her father still adhered to. Joelle knew that her best chance of influencing Beth for Christ would be to develop a close relationship with her. Rather than pushing her away, she needed to draw her in. So, Joelle asked God to help her do that and to give her opportunities to talk openly about her faith with Beth.

She and Beth became quite close and talked often about God, but Joelle didn't sense much progress being made spiritually. Several years passed. Beth became Joelle's daughter-in-law and their conversations about God continued, with no apparent fruit. Still, Joelle continued praying and listening.

One day it occurred to her that their conversations were always about God – not Jesus Christ specifically. Remembering Beth's background, Joelle became intentional about referring to Jesus by name. She noticed a subtle change in their conversations after that – a shy curiosity emerging through Beth's questions. More time passed until one day Beth made it clear she wanted to know Jesus Christ personally.

Joelle explained to Beth about Jesus' immense love for her and how He had died for her sins. What set Jesus Christ apart from all the other great men who have walked the face of the earth – what proves Jesus is God – is the fact that He was resurrected from the dead, Joelle explained to Beth. Beth absorbed every word and when Joelle asked if she wanted to receive Christ as her Savior, Beth said "yes" without hesitation.

After years of persistent, bold, beautiful witnessing, God answered Joelle's prayers! "I could scarcely believe what was happening," Joelle said. "After all those years of praying, after all those conversations, I'd pretty much given up hope. And then suddenly, there we were, praying together! My heart was beating out of my chest, I was so happy. God answered my prayers, but it was over the course of 12 years!"

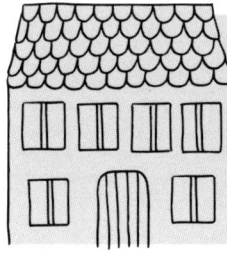

SCRIPTURE FOCUS

"Let us not become weary in doing good, for at the proper time we will reap a harvest if we do not give up" (Galatians 6:9).

Prayers for Yourself

Lord, help me to humble myself in Your sight and I know You will lift me up (James 4:10).

Lord, help me to always be joyful in hope, patient in affliction and faithful in prayer – especially as I pray for the salvation of my neighbors (Romans 12:12).

Father, help me always be prepared to give an answer to everyone who asks me about the reason for the hope I have in You, and help me do this with gentleness and respect (1 Peter 3:15).

Father, help me to lead a life worthy of Your calling, knowing that You have called me. Let me always be humble and gentle regarding my neighbors, patient with them, making allowance for their faults because of Your love (Ephesians 4:1-2, NLT).

Lord, help me never to tire of doing what is good (2 Thessalonians 3:13).

Thank you, Lord, for the promise that if I remain in You and Your words remain in me, I can ask whatever I wish, and You will give it to me according to Your will (John 15:7).

Prayers for Your Neighbors

Lord, let my neighbors come to You with their ears wide open. Let them listen and find life. Make an everlasting covenant with them and give them Your unfailing love (Isaiah 55:3, NLT).

Let my neighbors seek You while they can find You, Lord. Let them call on You while You are near. Lord, help them change their ways and turn to you so that You may have mercy on them and forgive them (Isaiah 55:6-7, NLT).

Reflections

What is God showing me today about my relationship with Him?

What is God showing me today about my relationship with my neighbors?

SECTION 3: OUR PRAYERS IN ACTION

SECTION 4:

Our

Hearts

Awakened

Avoiding Discouragement

Dave was devastated when he received a phone call that his lifelong mentor and friend, John, had just suffered a heart attack and was not expected to live. "John really stepped up to the plate after my father's death," Dave explained. "He helped me navigate my teen years and advised me through college and later as a businessman and family man. His support and friendship were priceless to me."

Thanks to his college roommate's influence, Dave had started a transformational relationship with Jesus Christ years before. But he was hesitant to share that experience with John at the time. "I didn't know what John would think about my decision," Dave explained, "because he'd never talked to me about God or, for that matter, anything spiritual."

When Dave did share his new faith with his mentor, John neither criticized nor supported the decision. He just made it clear it was not something that interested him. Over the next few years, Dave continued to share his faith with John, but he remained politely unpersuaded. Now, driving to the hospital where John fought for his life, Dave called a few close friends to pray as he prepared to share Jesus one last time with John.

In John's room in the hospital's intensive care unit, Dave reached through the tangle of life-sustaining tubes to hold John's hand. As the medical equipment beeped and hummed around them, Dave told John once again about his Savior, Jesus Christ. Unable to communicate, John focused his eyes on Dave's, but showed no visible sign that he heard or understood. When visiting time was almost over, Dave did something he had never done before in John's presence – he prayed.

Discouraged and heartsick, Dave returned home to find an email from one of the friends he had asked to pray. The message encouraged Dave and reminded him that his words to John weren't wasted. "John may be unable to respond to you," the friend's email said, "but he is not unable to respond to God. … God is putting to good use all you've said to him before and all you said today."

As humans, we are bound by earthly time. We can't escape the 24-hours-in-a-day, 365-days-in-a-year boundary of time. Nor can we see for certain beyond the precise second we are experiencing. The future is a question mark to us. But it isn't to God! He is not limited by the boundaries of time and space. He knows exactly what tomorrow holds for each of us just as clearly as we ourselves know what yesterday held.

In our human limitations, it is impossible to comprehend the ways of Sovereign God. "My thoughts are not your thoughts," He tells us in Isaiah 55:8, "and my ways are not your ways." But this one thing we know for sure: God's goodness governs His interactions with us. We must never lose hope that God is drawing to Himself those for whom we are praying.

Our prayers for the salvation of our neighbors are aligned with God's heart, and we are working in tandem with Him each time we carry out His commission to share the Gospel. Some people respond to Christ the first time they hear about Him, but for many more it is a process. They need to hear about Jesus' love for them again and again before the truth takes root. The process of coming to belief is unique to the individual.

The Bible paints a clear picture of this in Luke 8:1-15 with the parable of the sower. We can share the same message with four different people and they will hear it four different ways based on their background, personality, and current circumstances. All these things, and more, affect the way people hear our words.

Luke 8:4-8, NLT

4 One day Jesus told a story in the form of a parable to a large crowd that had gathered from many towns to hear him: 5 "A farmer went out to plant his seed. As he scattered it across his field, some seed fell on a footpath, where it was stepped on, and the birds ate it. 6 Other seed fell among rocks. It began to grow, but the plant soon wilted and died for lack of moisture. 7 Other seed fell among thorns that grew up with it and choked out the tender plants. 8 Still other seed fell on fertile soil. This seed grew and produced a crop that was a hundred times as much as had been planted!" When he had said this, he called out, "Anyone with ears to hear should listen and understand."

Read verses 4-8 and note the differences in the soil where the various seeds fell.

_____

_____

_____

_____

_____

Now read the meaning of the parable in verses 11-15 and draw comparisons to what you noted above. The seed the farmer sowed in this parable was the same each time. It just came to rest on different types of soil. And that's how it will be with the seeds of the Gospel we share with our neighbors. The seeds will fall in different ways. Some people will be ready to hear what we're saying, and some won't. Some will respond immediately; some won't. Some will flourish in their new-found truth, and for others the growth will be short-lived. How they respond is between them and God. What is between you and God is your faithfulness to spread the seed of God's Word to your neighborhood.

For this reason, do not measure your success or failure by how many of your neighbors begin a relationship with Christ as you share Him with them. That is not your primary responsibility. Only God can save. Only God draws people to

Himself. Do not be discouraged by what appears to be a lack of response. Just keep sharing faithfully, every opportunity you have. Share genuinely through your words and your actions. Leave the rest in God's hands.

Remember, you are one piece of the puzzle in your neighbor's faith journey. Others have been putting pieces in place as well. God brought your neighbor into your sphere of influence during this season for a purpose. Maybe you'll be the one to fit in the last piece, or maybe you'll be part of continuing to put the puzzle together. Regardless of your role, stay faithful and trust God.

SCRIPTURE FOCUS

"Before they call I will answer; while they are still speaking I will hear" (Isaiah 65:24).

Prayers for Yourself

How wonderful to know, Lord, that You will answer me before I even call on You. While I am still praying, You will go ahead and answer my prayers (Isaiah 65:24).

Father, help me to wait for You. Make me strong, and let my heart take courage as I wait for You (Psalm 27:14).

Father, help me to preach Your Word. Help me be prepared and keep a clear mind in every situation, unafraid of suffering for you. Help me always tell others the Good News and carry out the ministry You have given me. Let me be ready in season and out of season to preach Your Word (2 Timothy 4:1-5, NLT).

Father, I ask You to direct my heart to Your love and to the steadfastness of Christ (2 Thessalonians 3:5, ESV).

Prayers for Your Neighbors

Father, let the soil of my neighbor's heart be fertile. May You produce a crop that will be a hundred times as much as I have planted (Luke 8:8, NLT).

Father, I know that all who see the Son and believe in Him will have eternal life, and I ask this for my neighbors so that You will raise them up at the last day (John 6:40, NLT).

Lord, reveal Yourself to my neighbors. Give them ears to hear the truth (Mark 4:22).

Reflections

What is God showing me today about my relationship with Him?

What is God showing me today about my relationship with my neighbors?

The Importance of Discipleship

Shortly before He ascended to heaven, Jesus commissioned His disciples to share the Gospel with others. He said, "Go and make disciples of all nations … teaching them to obey everything I have commanded you" (Matthew 28:19-20). Notice that Jesus said to make disciples, implying an ongoing process of transformation rather than a one-time decision to follow Him. He stressed the importance of living a lifestyle of discipleship alongside new believers to help them learn God's ways.

In his book *The Body*, evangelical leader Chuck Colson, founder of Prison Fellowship, points out that "the verb tense of the commissioning of the disciples in Matthew's Gospel allows us to render Jesus' words literally, 'as you are going make disciples.' As you go. That means evangelism should flow naturally out of the context of our everyday lives. It's not a set of formulas, techniques, or memorized scenarios. It can't be put in a box. Evangelism is a consequence of holy living, [of] our own personal passion for Christ."[10]

As Colson explains, discipleship is part of God's Great Commission. The end goal after a decision to be a Christ-follower is that our neighbor will live life following Christ! We need to be prepared to continue sharing our faith journey and discipling those who begin a relationship with Jesus as a result of our prayers.

The joy of seeing our neighbors come to know Christ is compounded as we help them put roots down deep in God's love and truth. "When eyes are opened to see Christ the way He really is, and to see … the world and sin and righteousness and heaven and hell the way they really are, then … the power of Satan is broken by the Spirit of truth."[11] Jesus said, "If you hold to my teaching, you are really my disciples … and the truth will set you free" (John 8:31-32). Part of discipleship is helping our neighbors see themselves and their lives the way God does.

As their hearts are awakened to the transforming truth of the Gospel, new believers are often compelled to go and share their life-changing faith. That means your prayers for your neighbors today are sowing seeds that could multiply throughout your community over time, transforming hearts in every sphere of society. So, keep praying and sharing the Good News!

SCRIPTURE FOCUS

"Therefore go and make disciples of all nations, baptizing them in the name of the Father and of the Son and of the Holy Spirit, and teaching them to obey everything I have commanded you. And surely I am with you always, to the very end of the age" (Matthew 28:19-20).

Prayers for Yourself

Lord, give me grace to come alongside new believers in my community in teaching, fellowship, breaking of bread, and prayer (Acts 2:42).

Father, thank you that Christ in me is the hope of glory to my neighbors. May I teach others with Your wisdom so that we may become fully mature in Christ (Colossians 1:27-28).

As I take a step of faith in making disciples, Lord, I thank You for the promise that You are with me always, to the very end of the age (Matthew 28:20).

Prayers for Your Neighbors

Father, I ask You to draw people from every sphere of society in my community to become Your disciples. Teach them to obey Your commands and follow Your ways (Matthew 28:19-20).

Lord, thank You for being near to all who call on You in truth. Stir my neighbors' hearts today to seek the Truth that will set them free (Psalm 145:18, John 8:32).

Reflections

What is God showing me today about my relationship with Him?

What is God showing me today about my relationship with my neighbors?

SECTION 4: OUR HEARTS AWAKENED

God's Pursuing Love

We can expect God to give us opportunities to share the Gospel as we pray for our neighbors. This final section provides a sample guideline for what you might share in those conversations:

God, who created the universe, is full of love and mercy. He desires for you to personally receive His love and mercy.

It doesn't matter what has happened in your past. No matter what you've done, no matter what you regret about how you've lived your life, God's mercy is greater. God understands you – your hopes, your dreams, your frustrations, your loneliness, your heartaches. His love caused Him to pursue us, to leave heaven and come to Earth.

> For God so loved the world that he gave his one and only Son, that whoever believes in him shall not perish but have eternal life. For God did not send his Son into the world to condemn the world, but to save the world through him.
>
> - John 3:16-17

God is love. He is a God of relationship.

God created us to have a real and personal relationship with Him. Sin keeps us from having a loving relationship with God. We all have sinned and been separated from God. We all carry sin's consequences in our lives.

But God the Father loves so deeply that He made a way to close the gap of separation. He sent His Son Jesus to come to earth and live a perfect life with no sin and then to die in our place. Jesus Christ took the punishment for our sin. Jesus is God and He did the work for us.

Nothing we can do will earn us God's love. No good works. No good deeds. No avoidance of evil. "For God made Christ, who never sinned, to be the offering for our sin, so that we could be made right with God through Christ" (2 Corinthians 5:21).

> But God is so rich in mercy, and he loved us so much, that even though we were dead because of our sins, he gave us life when he raised Christ from the dead. (It is only by God's grace that you have been saved!)
>
> - Ephesians 2:4-5, NLT

Jesus Christ paid the penalty for sin when He died on the cross. But He did not stay dead! He came back to life. He rose from the dead. And He is ready to share His life with you.

Jesus is alive today. He offers reconciliation to us. He can give you a new beginning and a newly created life. "This means that anyone who belongs in Christ has become a new person. The old life is gone; a new life has begun!" (2 Corinthians 5:17, NLT).

How do you begin this new life? Place your trust in Jesus Christ. Believe that He is God and receive His love. Agree with God about your sin and believe that Jesus came to close the separation between you and God. Ask Jesus to lead your life.

When you trust Jesus Christ, He will live in your life. God's Spirit will live inside you. This Holy Spirit will help you live a life that honors Him.

Do you want to begin this new life? You can start today with a few simple words like, "Dear Jesus, I believe that You are God and that You love me and came to save me through Your death and resurrection."

Or you might pray something like this:

> *Jesus, I believe You are the Son of God and that You died on the cross to pay the penalty for my sin. Forgive me. I choose to turn away from my sin and live a life that honors You. I want to follow You and make You the leader of my life. Thank You for Your gift of eternal life and for the Holy Spirit who now has come to live in me. Amen.*

When a woman begins a relationship with Jesus Christ, Stonecroft wants to offer her a free publication called *A New Beginning*, a short Bible study that will help her get started on her new faith journey. She can order a free copy by filling out the form found on the lower part of this webpage: stonecroft.org/know-god. The form includes a small box to check to request a downloadable copy of *A New Beginning*. Also, please make sure she has a Bible. We recommend the New Living Translation (NLT).

May God move mightily in response to your prayers!

Reflections

What is God showing me today about my relationship with Him?

What is God showing me today about my relationship with my neighbors?

SECTION 4: OUR HEARTS AWAKENED

Group Prayer List

me

my neighbors

Leader's Guide

Every day, as God works through Stonecroft volunteers, women hear the Gospel – where they are, as they are. Stonecroft's volunteers and staff members are committed to sharing the Good News in relevant, meaningful ways with today's women. Prayer is vital to that work.

Stonecroft invests in resources that focus on prayer, along with excellent Bible studies, book studies, and other tools that communicate the Gospel. To learn more about these resources, visit stonecroft.org/store.

Stonecroft developed *Loving Your Neighbors* to help people gather in small groups to pray for their neighbors. As the leader, you have options on how you choose to facilitate the group time. Some suggestions are:

- Ensure that each participant has her own copy of *Loving Your Neighbors*. Visit stonecroft.org/store.

- The book is divided into four sections of three chapters each. Consider studying one chapter per group meeting to allow adequate time for discussion and prayer.

- Begin each group time by discussing the highlights of the chapter and interacting around the questions. The participants may want to read and write their responses before the meeting.

- After this short time of discussion, transition to prayer.

- Each chapter includes Scripture-based prayer for you and your neighbors. You may want to pray these out loud during the group or allow for silent prayer. Consider breaking into smaller, more intimate groups for prayer time.

- Each chapter ends with a section called "reflections," where participants can apply what they've heard from God through prayer. Consider asking a few participants to share their experience from the previous week.

Questions? Please contact us at connections@stonecroft.org or 800.525.8627. We are here to support you as you spend time loving and praying for your neighbors.

Who is Stonecroft

Every day Stonecroft volunteers communicate the Gospel in meaningful ways. Whether side-by-side with a neighbor or new friend, or through a speaker sharing her transformational story, the Gospel of Jesus Christ goes forward. Through a variety of outreach activities and small group Bible studies specifically designed for those not familiar with God, and with online and print resources focused on evangelism, Stonecroft proclaims the love of Jesus Christ to women where they are, as they are.

For more than 75 years, Stonecroft volunteers have found ways to introduce women to Jesus Christ and train them to share His Good News with others – always with a foundation of prayer and reliance on God.

Stonecroft understands and appreciates the influence of one woman's life. When we reach her, we touch everyone she knows – her family, friends, neighbors, and co-workers. The real truth of the Gospel brings real redemption into real lives.

Our life-changing, faith-building community resources include:

- Stonecroft Bible Studies

  We offer both topical and chapter-by-chapter studies. We designed Stonecroft studies for those in small groups to simply, yet profoundly, discover God's Word together.

- *Conversations*

  These thought-provoking small group resources engage women in conversation on topics that matter. Conversations include *Rest, Known,* and *Enough.*

- Stonecroft Prays

  This gathering helps small groups of women pray for God to show them avenues to reach women in their community with the Gospel.

- Outreach Events

    These set the stage for women to hear and share the Gospel with their communities. Whether in a large venue, workshop, or small group setting, Stonecroft women find ways to share the love of Christ.

- Stonecroft Military

    This specialized effort honors women connected to the U.S. military and shares with them the Gospel while showing them the love of Christ.

- Stonecroft Aware Series

    These resources reveal God's heart for those who do not yet know Him. The Aware Series includes *Aware, Belong,* and *Call.*

- stonecroft.org

    Our website offers fresh content daily to equip and encourage you.

Dedicated and enthusiastic Stonecroft staff and volunteers serve together to engage women in sharing the love of Christ with the world. Your life matters. Join us today to become part of reaching your communities with the Gospel of Jesus Christ. Become involved with Stonecroft.

Resources

Ephesians: Made Complete in Christ
Reflect on the big love of God and find His strength and power to live victoriously.

7 chapters

Discovering the Joy of Jesus
This study of Philippians helps you find joy, regardless of your circumstances.

9 chapters

You Are Alive in Christ
Explore Colossians and discover our intimate relationship with Christ.

8 chapters

God's Love Through You
The book of 1 John begins and ends talking about a fulfilling, meaningful life.

9 chapters

Rest
This conversation helps you discover how God enables us to find rest in an overly busy world.

4 conversations

Known
Achievements and appearance don't determine real worth. Instead, find love and acceptance in God's eyes.

4 conversations

Enough
God helps us embrace who we really are, rather than fear what we're missing.

4 conversations

Order at stonecroft.org/store or call 888.819.5218.

Notes

[1] Palmer, Earl. *The Book that John Wrote*, (Vancouver, BC, Canada: Regent College Publishing, 1999), 146.

[2] "Plesion," http://www.biblestudytools.com. Accessed July 05, 2017. http://www.biblestudytools.com/lexicons/greek/nas/plesion.html.

From *The New Testament Greek Lexicon (New American Standard)*, available on http://www.biblestudytools.com.

[3] Piper, John. "Love your Neighbor as Yourself" (part 1), http://www.desiringgod.org. Sermon posted on April 30, 1995. Accessed July 17, 2017. http://www.desiringgod.org/messages/love-your-neighbor-as-yourself-part-1.

[4] Cymbala, Jim. *Fresh Power,* (Grand Rapids, Michigan: Zondervan, 2003), 20-22.

[5] Zeiler, Jean Lovelace. *Like a Pebble Tossed*, (Nashville, Tennessee: ACW Press, 2001), 94-96.

[6] Adams, Mark. "Attitudes Essential for Evangelism," http://www.redlandbaptist.org. A sermon posted on May 30, 2004. Accessed July 05, 2017. http://www.redlandbaptist.org/sermon/attitudes-essential-to-evangelism.

A sermon by Mark Adams, citing material from *Just Walk Across the Room*, a book by Bill Hybels.

[7] Richardson, Rick. *Reimagining Evangelism*, (Westmont, Illinois: InterVarsity Press, 2006), 97.

[8] Baugh, Helen Duff, founder of Stonecroft Ministries. Sermon notes.

[9] Lotz, Anne Graham. *The Joy of My Heart: Meditating Daily on God's Word*, (Nashville, Tennessee: Thomas Nelson, 2004), 21.

[10] Colson, Charles and Vaughn, Ellen Santilli. *The Body*, (Nashville, Tennessee: Thomas Nelson, 1994), 91, 328-329.

[11] Ibid.

Surgery

Cardiovascular System

Hemodialysis Access, Intervascular Cannulation for Extracorporeal Circulation, or Shunt Insertion

The first CPT Assistant reference following code 36822, which reads "Fall 93:3;" should be deleted.

Female Genital System

Vagina

ENDOSCOPY

The cross-reference following the "Endoscopy" heading which references the Category III codes for speculoscopy should state:

(For speculoscopy, see Category III codes 0031T, 0032T)

CPT 2003 Index

After **Tympanomastoidectomy**—add **See Tympanoplasty**